V&A Pattern
Spitalfields Silks

V&A Publishing

V&A Pattern

Spitalfields Silks

First published by V&A Publishing, 2011
V&A Publishing
Victoria and Albert Museum
South Kensington
London SW7 2RL

Distributed in North America by Harry N. Abrams, Inc., New York

ISBN 978 1 85177 635 1
Library of Congress Control Number 2010937392

10 9 8 7 6 5 4 3 2 1
2015 2014 2013 2012 2011

A catalogue record for this book is available
from the British Library.

Series Art Direction: Rose
Design: TurnbullGrey www.turnbullgrey.co.uk

Front cover (A):
Anna Maria Garthwaite, design for a silk
Pencil, watercolour and bodycolour on paper. UK, *c.*1730 (V&A: 5975:4)
Pages 2–3 (B):
James Leman, design for a silk
Pencil, watercolour and bodycolour on paper. UK, *c.*1721 (V&A: E.4450–1909)
Page 6 (C):
James Leman, design for a silk
Pencil, pen and ink, watercolour and bodycolour on paper. UK, 1706–7 (V&A: E.1861:35–1991)
Page 11 (D):
Anna Maria Garthwaite, design for a silk
Pencil, watercolour and bodycolour on paper. UK, 1733 (V&A: 5975:17)
Pages 78–9 (E):
Batchelor, Ham & Perigal, sample from a pattern book
Woven silk, 1782 (V&A: T.377:69–1972)

Letters (in brackets) refer to the file name of the images on the accompanying disc.

Printed in China

V&A Publishing
Victoria and Albert Museum
South Kensington
London SW7 2RL
www.vandabooks.com

V&A Pattern

Each *V&A Pattern* book is an introduction to the Victoria and Albert Museum's extraordinarily diverse collection. The museum has more than three million designs for textiles, decorations, wallpapers and prints; some well-known, others less so. This series explores pattern-making in all its forms, across the world and through the centuries. The books are intended to be both beautiful and useful – showing patterns to enjoy in their own right and as inspiration for new design.

V&A Pattern presents the greatest names and styles in design, while also highlighting the work of anonymous draughtsmen and designers, often working unacknowledged in workshops, studios and factories, and responsible for designs of aesthetic originality and technical virtuosity. Many of the most interesting and imaginative designs are seen too rarely. *V&A Pattern* gathers details from our best objects and hidden treasures from pattern books, swatch books, company archives, design records and catalogues to form a fascinating introduction to the variety and beauty of pattern at the V&A.

The compact disc at the back of each book invites you to appreciate the ingenuity of the designs, and the endless possibilities for their application. To use the images professionally, you need permission from V&A Images, as the V&A controls – on behalf of others – the rights held in its books and CD-Roms. *V&A Pattern* can only ever be a tiny selection of the designs available at www.vandaimages.com. We see requests to use images as an opportunity to help us to develop and improve our licensing programme – and for us to let you know about images you may not have found elsewhere.

Spitalfields Silks
Moira Thunder

In the eighteenth-century the area of Spitalfields, which was then just north of London's walls, was a major centre for European silk weaving. Weavers there produced silks that were among the most expensive and fashionable dress fabrics of the times, and this book includes a selection of the watercolour designs and woven silks they made from the early eighteenth century to the mid-1820s.

Located close to court – then the epicentre of fashion – Spitalfields weavers absorbed the latest styles as they were introduced by diplomats and other visitors from the continent. While the tailoring and cuts of dress changed slowly, the patterns woven into the silks changed seasonally and ultimately determined garments' fashionability. Portraits made between 1713 and 1750 show British and European royalty and nobility wearing rich silks, often brocaded in gold and silver threads, while the gentry and members of wealthy families are depicted in plainer styles. Mercers, or retailers, based in Ludgate Hill and Covent Garden commissioned silks from Spitalfields weavers, who in turn delegated some of the actual weaving to their journeymen. The mercers then sold the silks on to their rich and fashionable clientele, whose tailors or servants produced the desired garments.

Many silk weavers in England were French Huguenots who, having fled persecution in France, began to trade in Spitalfields; they include James Leman (*c.*1688–1745) and Christopher Baudouin (*c.*1665–1736), whose designs are shown here.

Indigenous talent is represented by English pattern drawers Joseph Dandridge (1660–1746) and Anna Maria Garthwaite (1690–1763). Spitalfields weavers, regardless of national background, all faced stiff competition from France, particularly from weavers based in Lyons. French innovations in weaving technology resulted in high-quality silks with wonderful designs that challenged the English industry's growth. By 1766, however, isolationist acts passed by government had banned textile imports to protect the silk industry from foreign competition. As a result, the Spitalfields silk industry flourished and even exported to the American colonies.

While Leman was both a designer and master weaver, most designers in the trade were independent pattern drawers who focused solely on creating patterns. Such work, however, still demanded a thorough understanding of the weaving process in order to produce patterns that were at once attractive *and* feasible. Different types of metal threads were identified by using strong reds and yellows as colour codes (plates 9 and 12). Another professional, who was not normally the pattern drawer in eighteenth-century England, but could be by the early 1800s, transferred the design onto ruled paper divided into squares corresponding to the warp and weft threads of a woven textile. The pattern was thus enlarged four to six times the scale of the original so that the individual threads became visible. The professional then applied bodycolour transparent enough to show the grid beneath the layer of colour. From the resulting ruled design, a 'reader' (*liseuse* in France) instructed a lash maker which lashes or loops of cord to tie around the relevant piece of the loom, enabling the weaver to produce the desired pattern. Different weaving techniques produced various types of textile, such as damask brocaded in coloured silks (plate 4) or satin ground brocaded with gold threads and details in coloured silks (plate 28).

In the mid-twentieth century, textile historians took to describing patterns produced between 1700 and 1710 as 'bizarre' because of their strange shapes and combinations of motifs (plates 4, 6 and 8). These styles evolved into what was later termed a 'luxuriant' phase, with patterns resembling jungle vegetation (plates 22 and 23), followed thereafter by patterns featuring ornamental surrounds that enclose symmetrical point repeats (plates 32 and 34). Between 1720 and 1732, designs with patterned areas similar to lace became popular (plate 42), but then fashions changed again when the introduction of skirts stretched over wide hoops led to a demand for larger motifs.

By 1742, heavy forms were replaced by a new naturalism that broke from such styles. These distinctly English patterns featured floral sprigs – often identifiable flowers such as carnations and auricula (plates 49, 50, 51 and 52) – scattered lightly over a pale ground. They reflected the English love of gardens and remained popular throughout the 1740s and early 1750s. In the mid-1750s, patterns still featured light arrangements but with motifs woven in metal threads acting as foils to flowers (plates 57 and 58). Smaller patterns featuring sprigs and natural forms, including scallop shells, came into favour, such as those probably produced by the firm Batchelor, Ham & Perigal (plates 60 and 61). Spitalfields silks continue to have enduring appeal today and those original textile firms that survive often turn to their company archives to locate centuries-old designs and textiles that still astonish observers with their éclat.

1
James Leman, design for a silk
Pencil, pen and ink, watercolour and bodycolour on paper. UK, 1706–7 (V&A: E.1861:15–1991)

2
James Leman, design for a silk
Pencil, pen and ink, watercolour and bodycolour on paper. UK, 1707 (V&A: E.1861:6–1991)

3
James Leman, design for a silk
Pencil, pen and ink, watercolour and bodycolour on paper. UK, 1707 (V&A: E.1861:46–1991)

4
Dress fabric
Woven silk damask brocaded with coloured silks. UK, *c.*1707–8 (V&A: 711–1864)

5
James Leman, design for a silk
Pencil, pen and ink, and watercolour on paper. UK, 1710 (V&A: E.1861:84–1991)

6
James Leman, design for a silk
Pencil, pen and ink, and watercolour on paper. UK, 1710 (V&A: E.1861:72–1991)

7
James Leman, design for a silk
Pencil, pen and ink, and watercolour on paper. UK, 1709 (V&A: E.1861:95–1991)

8
Dress fabric
Woven satin with patterning wefts of silver thread. UK, *c.*1708 (V&A: T.3–1994)

9
James Leman, design for a silk
Pencil, pen and ink, and watercolour on paper. UK, 1717 (V&A: E.4440–1909)

10
James Leman, design for a silk
Pencil, pen and ink, and bodycolour on paper. UK, 1720 (V&A: E.4456–1909)

11
James Leman, design for a silk
Pencil, pen and ink, watercolour and bodycolour on paper. UK, *c.*1719 (V&A: E.4517–1909)

12
Joseph Dandridge, design for a silk
Pencil and watercolour on paper. UK, 1718 (V&A: E.4466–1909)

13
James Leman, design for a silk
Pencil, pen and ink, watercolour and bodycolour on paper. UK, 1720 (V&A: E.4459–1909)

14
Joseph Dandridge, design for a silk
Pencil, pen and ink, and watercolour on paper. UK, 1720 (V&A: E.4514–1909)

15
Joseph Dandridge, design for a silk
Pencil, pen and ink, and watercolour on paper. UK, 1720 (V&A: E.4453–1909)

16
James Leman, design for a silk
Pencil, pen and ink, and watercolour on paper. UK, 1721 (V&A: E.4455–1909)

17
Probably James Leman, design for a silk
Pencil, watercolour and bodycolour on paper. UK, 1719 (V&A: E.4443–1909)

18
Joseph Dandridge, design for a silk
Pencil, pen and ink, and watercolour on paper. UK, 1720 (V&A: E.4518–1909)

19
James Leman, design for a silk
Pencil, pen and ink, watercolour and bodycolour on paper. UK, 1718 (V&A: E.4468–1909)

20
James Leman, design for a silk
Pencil, pen and ink, watercolour and bodycolour on paper. UK, 1720 (V&A: E.4503–1909)

21
James Leman, design for a silk
Pencil, watercolour and bodycolour on paper. UK, 1719 (V&A: E.4472–1909)

22
James Leman, design for a silk
Pencil, pen and ink, watercolour and bodycolour on paper. UK, 1719 (V&A: E.4511–1909)

23
James Leman, design for a silk
Pencil, pen and ink, and watercolour on paper. UK, 1721 (V&A: E.4446–1909)

24
James Leman, design for a silk
Pencil, pen and ink, watercolour and bodycolour on paper. UK, 1720 (V&A: E.4484–1909)

25
Joseph Dandridge, design for a silk
Pencil, watercolour and bodycolour on paper. UK, 1720 (V&A: E.4441–1909)

26
Joseph Dandridge, design for a silk
Pencil, pen and ink, watercolour and bodycolour on paper. UK, 1721 (V&A: E.4505–1909)

27
Possibly James Leman, design for a silk
Pencil, watercolour and bodycolour on paper. UK, 1726–9 (V&A: 5973:16)

28
Segment from George II's Coronation Canopy
Woven satin brocaded with gold thread and coloured silks. UK, 1726–7 (V&A: T.184–1975)

29
Christopher Baudouin, design for a silk
Pencil and watercolour on paper. UK, 1723–4 (V&A: 5973:17)

30
Robe
Woven satin patterned in coloured silks. UK, 1725–30 (V&A: T.180–1962)

31
Anna Maria Garthwaite, design for a silk
Pencil, watercolour and bodycolour on paper. UK, *c.*1732 (V&A: 5975:8)

32
Christening mantle
Woven silk brocaded with coloured silks. UK, *c.*1728 (V&A: T.76–1936)

33
Christopher Baudouin, design for a silk
Pencil, pen and ink, and watercolour on paper. UK, *c.*1726 (V&A: 5973:6)

34
Dress fabric
Woven silk brocaded with coloured silks. UK, 1724–5 (V&A: T.18–1969)

35
Anna Maria Garthwaite, design for a silk
Pencil and watercolour on paper. UK, 1726–7 (V&A: 5970:3)

36
Anna Maria Garthwaite, design for a silk
Pencil and watercolour on paper. UK, 1726–7 (V&A: 5970:16)

37
Anna Maria Garthwaite, design for a silk
Pencil and watercolour on paper. UK, *c.*1726 (V&A: 5970:11)

38
Anna Maria Garthwaite, design for a silk
Pencil and watercolour on paper. UK, 1726–8 (V&A: 5970:21)

39
Anna Maria Garthwaite, design for a silk
Pencil, pen and ink, and watercolour on paper. UK, *c.*1726 (V&A: 5970:1)

40
Anna Maria Garthwaite, design for a silk
Pencil, pen and ink, and watercolour on paper. UK, 1727 (V&A: 5970:46)

41
Anna Maria Garthwaite, design for a silk
Pencil and watercolour on paper. UK, 1733 (V&A: 5975:9)

42
Anna Maria Garthwaite, design for a silk
Pencil and watercolour on paper. UK, *c.*1730 (V&A: 5975:2)

43
Dress fabric
Woven silk brocaded with silver thread and coloured silks. UK, *c.*1734 (V&A: T.26–1966)

44
Dress fabric
Woven silk brocaded with coloured silks. UK, *c.*1734 (V&A: T.99–1912)

45
Anna Maria Garthwaite, design for a silk
Pencil, watercolour and bodycolour on paper. UK, 1738 (V&A: 5977:11)

46
Dress fabric
Woven silk brocaded with coloured silks. UK, *c.*1740 (V&A: T.347–1910)

47
Anna Maria Garthwaite, design for a silk
Pencil, watercolour and bodycolour on paper. UK, 1741 (V&A: 5979:6)

48
Anna Maria Garthwaite, design for a silk
Pencil, pen and ink, watercolour and bodycolour on paper. UK, 1742 (V&A: 5980:13)

49
Anna Maria Garthwaite, design for a silk (see also plate 50)
Pencil, pen and ink, watercolour and bodycolour on paper. UK, 1747 (V&A: 5985:2)

50
Possibly Daniel Vautier, gown (see also plate 49)
Woven silk tobine brocaded with coloured silks. UK, 1747 (V&A: T.706–1913)

51
Anna Maria Garthwaite, design for a silk (see also plate 52)
Pencil, pen and ink, and watercolour on paper. UK, 1744 (V&A: 5982:10)

52
Gown (see also plate 51)
Woven satin brocaded with coloured silks. UK, 1744 (V&A: T.264–1966)

53
Anna Maria Garthwaite, design for a silk (see also plate 54)
Pencil, pen and ink, and watercolour on paper. UK, 1747 (V&A: 5985:9)

54
Possibly Daniel Vautier, dress (see also plate 53)
Woven silk lustring brocaded with coloured silks. UK, 1747 (V&A: T.720–1913)

55
Anna Maria Garthwaite, design for a silk (see also plate 56)
Pencil, pen and ink, and watercolour on paper. UK, 1749 (V&A: 5987:1)

56
Possibly Daniel Vautier (see also plate 55)
Woven silk tobine brocaded with coloured silks. UK, 1749 (V&A: T.192–1996)

57
Dress fabric
Woven silk brocaded with silver-gilt thread and coloured silks. UK, 1750–55 (V&A: Circ.513–1931)

58
Dress fabric
Woven silk brocaded with silver thread and coloured silks. UK, 1750–60 (V&A: T.161A–1959)

59
Dress fabric
Woven silk brocaded with coloured silks. UK, 1744–7 (V&A: T.147–1973)

60
Probably Batchelor, Ham & Perigal, sample from a pattern book
Woven silk tobine. UK, *c.*1755–65 (V&A: T.375:17–1972)

61
Probably Batchelor, Ham & Perigal, samples from a pattern book
Woven silk in different colourways. UK, 1763–5 (V&A: T.375:311–1972)

62
Batchelor, Ham & Perigal, samples from a pattern book
Woven silk in different colourways. UK, 1768–80 (V&A: T.374:1–1972)

63
Jourdain and John Ham, sample from a pattern book
Woven silk in different colourways. UK, 1816–26 (V&A: T.385:154–1972)

64
Jourdain and John Ham, samples from a pattern book
Woven silk in different colourways. UK, 1816–26 (V&A: T.385:189–1972)

65
Sample from a pattern book
Woven silk in different colourways. UK, 1816–26 (V&A: T.385:121–1972)

66
Jourdain and John Ham, sample from a pattern book
Woven silk in different colourways. UK, 1816–26 (V&A: T.385:250–1972)

Further Reading

Browne, Clare
'The Influence of Botanical Sources on Early 18th-Century English Silk Design'
in *Eighteenth-Century Silks: The Industries of England and Northern Europe*
Riggisberg, 2000 (pp.25–38)

Miller, Lesley Ellis
'Between Engraving and Silk Manufacture in Late Eighteenth-Century Lyons: Marie-Anne Bernier and Other Point Papermakers'
in *Studies in the Decorative Arts* Vol.3, 1995–6 (pp. 52–76)

Parry, Linda, intro.
British Textiles: 1700 to the Present
London, 2010

Rothstein, Natalie
Silk Designs of the Eighteenth Century in the Collection of the Victoria and Albert Museum
London, 1990

Thornton, Peter
Baroque and Rococo Silks
London, 1965

Digital Images

The patterns reproduced in this book are stored on the accompanying compact disc as jpeg files (at approximately A5-size, 300 dpi). You should be able to open them, and manipulate them, direct from the CD-ROM in most modern image software (on Windows or Mac platforms), and no installation should be required (although we, as publishers, cannot guarantee absolutely that the disk will be accessible for every computer).

Instructions for tracing and tiling the images will be found with the documentation for your software.

The names of the files correspond to the V&A inventory numbers of the images.